This book belongs to:

Please sign here:_____

and here:_____

and here:_____

Santa's Tooting Tooshie

by Humor Heals Us

Santa's work began on the strike of Christmas Eve.

But visiting that many houses meant he had to have extra energy. Fortunately, Mrs. Claus packed his favorite snacks on board the sleigh.

Tacos, burgers, mini pizzas, burritos, and even spicy chips. And sometimes, that would only last a few hours.

Eating that much food meant Santa had a lot of gas. His tooting tooshie served a purpose though. As you'll soon find out...

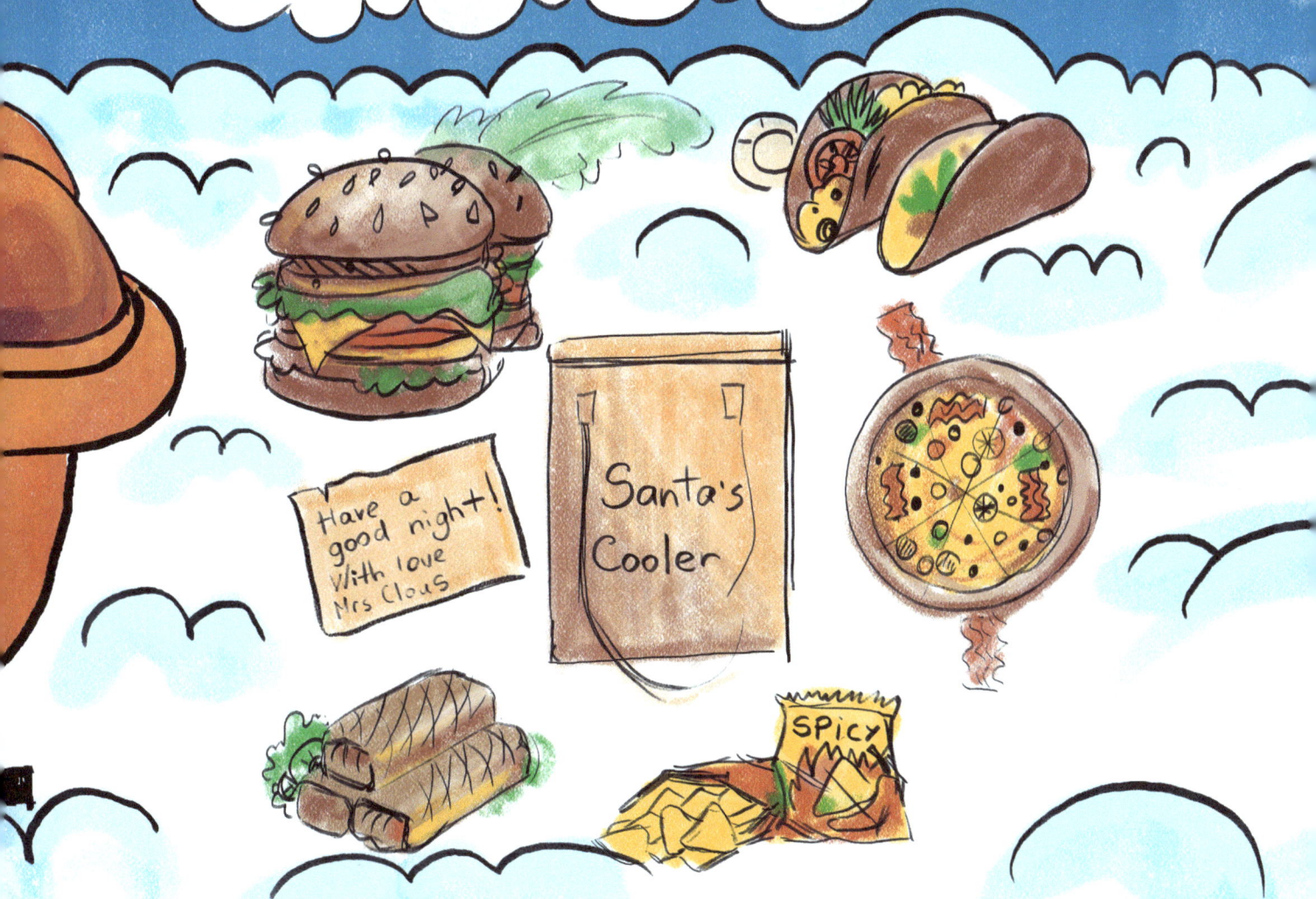

Have a good night!
With love
Mrs Claus

Santa's Cooler

SPICY

When Rudolph's red nose got dim and the crew needed more light, the reindeers shouted…

"Toot, Santa!"

So Santa released **toot torches**.

When air traffic got busy, the reindeers shouted…

"Toot, Santa!"

And Santa would **toot traffic lights** out.

On rare occasions, some kids didn't have a Christmas tree so he released a **toot tree** and placed the presents gingerly underneath. Thank goodness the children were asleep and the air was clean by morning!

Some houses had so many kids in it that Santa created a **toot truck** just to help bring in the extra load.

Sometimes, it was hard for Santa to get up and down the chimney so he called upon his **toot tools**.

SANTA'S TOOLS

To keep his reindeer excited throughout the long night, he summoned a toot TV and played their favorite movies. Mostly about super reindeers.

In really dark areas of the sky, he released a **toot track** so he could see the route better.

Even though the team checked and packed the gifts carefully for each boy and girl, sometimes there would be a gift or two missing.

On these rare occasions, Santa called upon his **talented elf toots**. They would craft a toy right there on the spot.

If one of the reindeer got injured, Santa made a self-driving **toot taxi** to take him home.

On the way back to the North Pole, Santa constructed a **telegram toot** to send Mrs. Claus a message that he was headed back.

Can't wait to see you. Thank you for all my snacks. They really helped!!! Next time I could probably use a dozen more.

And that's how Santa's tooting tooshie helped us all on Christmas Eve!

Follow us on FB and IG @humorhealsus
To vote on new title names and freebies, visit us
at humorhealsus.com for more information.

@humorhealsus   @humorhealsus

www.ingramcontent.com/pod-product-compliance
Lightning Source LLC
Chambersburg PA
CBHW042026090426
42811CB00016B/1751